Counting Backwards

From Gone

KAT SAVAGE

Counting Backwards From Gone

Copyright © 2019 Kat Savage

Cover Design by Kat Savage
Edited by Christina Hart

ISBN: 9781694163226

Also by Kat Savage

With This Lie: A Novel

For Now: A Novel

Poetry:

I Hope This Makes You Uncomfortable

This is How I Die

Throes

Redamancy

Anchors & Vacancies

Mad Woman

Learning To Speak

Co-Authored with J.R. Rogue:

Secrets We Told The City

A note from the author:

This is my raw, unfiltered grief.
This is how I feel, the weight of my loss.
I would encourage you to read the numbered
titles as part of the poem, with significance.
They are important.

For Angela,
my little sister, my love.
My heart is not the same without you.
I miss you terribly. I am so sorry.

Every year on your birthday
I think about making a chocolate cake.
I think about getting some balloons,
lighting a candle,
releasing the balloons into the sky
and silently wishing you happiness.

Every year, I can't bring myself
to go through with it.
My eyes open that morning
already brimming with tears.
I can already feel the sting
in my lungs.

Everyone around me knows
what today is.
They know why my eyes are red,
cheeks puffy.
They tilt their head at me,
hand me a tissue,
say they're sorry.

I wipe my swollen face,
listen to sad songs,
wallow in the empty space
of your memories
and I am scared.

Your face in my mind
is fading,
and I'm forgetting
what you sounded like
when you would say you love me,
when you would laugh.

I am afraid that one day,
I will wake up on your birthday
and I won't be able to remember
you
at all.
I am afraid I will wake up
and mourn you all over again.

17

I am braiding the
long blonde hair of your daughter
and as it falls between my fingers
I am reminded of all the times
you had me do this to
your long blonde hair.

She tells me she misses you
and I realize she probably only
misses the idea of you,
probably only misses
what we have told her,
what we have attempted
to have live on about you.

I tell her I miss you too,
that I think about you each night,
regale childhood memories
and watch her eyes light up.

I cannot replace you,
wouldn't even try.
I hold her tightly,
love her as you did,
as you would have.

But it will never be the same,
it will never still the yearning
inside her for her mother,

for a heart so close to hers,
it might as well be hers.

Our little sister is so angry,
angry at everyone,
angry at him.
She is blinded with a need
for revenge,
a need to play this in reverse.

She wants to unmourn you,
she wants to unwrap her arms
from our mother,
uncry the tears,
the salt we cannot get back
from the earth.

She wants to go back,
hear your smile from
across the room,
watch your words echo
through her.

All this time later
and I still don't have
the heart to tell her
we cannot get you
back from the earth
either.

Our mother wouldn't talk about you
and your dad wouldn't stop talking
about you
and somewhere in the middle
I couldn't breathe.

I have been taking half breaths
since the moment you took
your last breath.
Tears stained my green dress
that morning.
I haven't been able
to wear it again
but I haven't been able
to throw it away either.

Sometimes I walk into my closet,
stare at it for several moments,
relive it,
close my eyes and see myself
all those years ago,
just moments before I found out.

In that moment,
I am carefree, I am happy,
I am stupid and oblivious.
I wonder how I didn't know,
how I couldn't feel it.

Guilt washes over me
as I stand in my closet,
smelling the salt and regret
on my dress.

You were taken
the day before Thanksgiving
and so each year as
people prepare to gather
around mounds of food,
ready for their gluttonous fill,
ready to hold hands,
pray, and give their thanks,
I stand in the middle of
the grocery store aisle
staring down at a can of
cranberry sauce in my hand
and try not to panic.

In the next aisle,
I collect bags of stuffing mix
and see a petite girl
with long blonde hair
and I could swear she is you.
I want to tap her on the shoulder,
swing her around on her heels,
and see your face.

You are a ghost
standing next to a freezer full
of turkeys,
a cold chill down my spine
as I collect potatoes and onions,

the hair on the back of my neck
that stands on end
in the baking aisle.

I pour a glass of wine,
sip it over the stove,
searching inside myself
for something,
anything
for which to be grateful.

No one tells you
how difficult it is
to see past the pain,
to feel anything else.

13

Our mother died on a Saturday,
three years and three months after you,
but one year and three months
before he finally paid for taking you.

I stood in court for both of you that day,
addressed him with my biggest voice,
said all the things I needed to say,
all the things Mom would have wanted to say.

I can't think of a more painful way to die
than that of a mother with a broken heart.
The death certificate might read
"accidental overdose"
but her face begged the stars each night
to take her under,
to never give her back,
to let her go home to you.

He took two that night,
he took two.

I hope she got to come home to you.
Tell her I miss her.

You would have been thirty
this year and
I would have liked to have seen you
· with gray in your temples,
with laugh lines forming around
your crystal blue eyes.

I wonder what kind of job
you'd be working,
what kind of car you'd be driving,
if you'd have lived close enough to
come over for week-day dinners.

I wonder if you'd have quit smoking,
what sort of hobbies you'd have settled into,
if you'd still be able to eat your weight
in steak and baked potatoes.

Which is to say
I wonder about the most mundane things,
the things that would have made up
a normal life,
a life that can never be lived,
a life cut too short.

My mind cycles up a memory
of your ugly little toes digging into
mud at the edge of that mucky pond
in the woods behind the house.

Dirt is caked under your nails,
your hair a stringy mess,
your knees scuffed,
your shirt stained.

You're smiling brilliant white,
perfect straight teeth even in your youth,
laughing through them,
a cackle echoing through the trees.

I fall and cut my knee,
tears streaking down my
dirty pink cherub cheeks.

You sit down beside me and put your
head against my shoulder,
consoling me and cursing the
neighbor's dog who knocked me down.

I am back here now,
rubbing my chest as though
it's wounded and wondering
how I am to survive a life
without you,

without your head on my shoulder
ever again.

People ask me how I deal with the grief,
how I am surviving it.

People try to say time heals;
people try to say the grief grows smaller.

I tell them
loss is a bucket of stones I carry with me,
drag around behind me,
and no rocks fall out.

I tell them the bucket doesn't get smaller
or lighter
and I never put it down.

I tell them it only feels easier to carry
because I have carried it for so long.
I tell them I am stronger now
than I was in the days following.

They don't understand it
because they don't have their own
bucket of rocks.

The weight of a loss
is with you always,
always daring you to
lie down, to quit.

For you,
I will never give up.

9

I couldn't save you from him
and this is my biggest regret.

I think about what it must have
been like for you.

Were you scared?
Did you feel it?

When he took you from this world,
did you go quietly
or
did you fight back?

My mind is a canvas of unanswered questions
and he refuses to give us
the peace that comes with knowing.

The truth is with you,
in the stars,
a wisp of a life that once was.

The truth is with him,
held tight to his chest,
his lips sealed,
the last pain he can deliver.
I only hope it eats away
at his insides,

that the corrosion of what he did
is what finally kills him.

8

Sometimes life
feels like an endless
succession of Novembers,
each one darker and colder
than the one before it.

Sometimes I don't remember
anything but that day,
leaves turning,
crisp in the air.

I miss you,
in case I haven't said it.
I miss everything about you.

The cigarette between your fingers,
the glass of Mountain Dew
in your other hand,
your mid-drift shirt
riding up your back,
exposing the edge of the tattoo
you'd started.

I miss your lanky arms
stretched tight around me,
your hugs so tight and tender
despite your petite stature.

I miss you,
the whole of you,

the essence of you,
you.

7

I've only ever said his name
out loud
into the world
two times.

Once when someone asked,
again when I wrote it down.

Most days I forget it entirely,
let it fall out of my mind
as quickly and insignificantly
as this week's
winning lottery numbers.

People talk about repressing things,
about self-preservation,
and maybe that's why I can't remember it
but I don't try,
I will it out of me,
as if holding onto it
is a betrayal to you.

For him to take up space inside me
is more than I can manage.

He doesn't deserve more
of my time,
my energy,
my thoughts.

He doesn't deserve to be remembered,
or have his name spoken,
or hear anyone is thinking of him.

Even now,
I'm sad I wasted this paper and ink
on him.

6

The middle gets a little fuzzy now,
and I see glimpses of
sad songs playing in my car,
having to leave work on the anniversary
of your murder because
every move I make hurts too much.

I trace your name engraved on
the top of the wooden box
that contains your ashes,
run my fingers over the dried roses
tucked inside next to you.

I pull your handwritten letters
from a file folder where I keep
important documents
and run my thumb over the ink
of your signed name,
imagining you concentrating hard
on what you needed to say.

I make myself a sandwich,
cheese on toast,
the sandwich you always ate,
the only thing I could force myself
to eat for days after you'd gone.

Life is, in some ways,
in a state of perpetual

slow motion,
my heart too fragile
to move faster.

5

People begin to whitewash
life,
tucking away any reminder of you,
because for them
pretending you never surrounded us
is easier than accepting
you were once here
and then pulled away so violently
it left a rip in the seams.

We folded your clothes,
put them into tubs in the basement
because as much as Mom
couldn't look at them,
she couldn't let them go either.

Your photos are gathered together,
boxed for safe keeping,
boxed for safe looking around.

I am angry now
and I need people to stop
asking me if I'm okay
because the answer will never change.

I am not okay,
will never be okay again,
I struggle between wanting to
keep your memory alive

and needing to whitewash
like the others.

4

Everyone walks around,
a shell of who they were,
quiet and somber
and zombie-like.

Shock and ache
and a hint of anger
have washed over
our faces,
fixed there with a permanency,
never to be wiped away.

I can't breathe in deep anymore;
my lungs are a shallow shadow
of what they used to be,
barely functioning.

I hear a pain
in any voice that mutters
your name;
it comes out like a cry,
a plea,
like if we beg
long enough and loud enough
everything will reset.

3

We learn about him,
his name,
what he confessed doing.

We see his face light up
our television screen,
printed in black dots
across the newspaper,
in a Google search of
your name.

We watch as he
recants his confession,
washes his hands of blood
and wrongdoing.

We hear another story,
one about how his
memories of that night
have washed from his mind,
have gone out with the tide
of the moon on that night.

We watch him sit in a jail cell,
warm, belly full.
We watch him live on.

We counted on our fingers
and toes the years
and months

and days it took
to finally watch him walk
across the courtroom
and pay a price.

He didn't pay enough,
will spend the rest of his life
coming up short,
will live to see days he doesn't
deserve,
will sleep,
will eat,
will laugh,
will cry,
will live
a life
he doesn't
deserve.

Our mother was rocking
back and forth
on her bathroom floor,
refusing the truth as easily
as someone brushing off
the inconvenience of
an unseasonal rain.

Her face was an expression
both blank and afraid,
afraid of the truth,
afraid of this reality,
a reality where someone
had taken what
she had given life to.

She begged us to make sure
you weren't just sleeping,
to shake you hard and
just make sure,
because you were always
so difficult to wake.

I sat down beside her,
gently stroking her hair,
uncradling the truth I carried
in my arms,
held tight to my chest.

I looked into her eyes,
puffy and wild,
poured from my mouth
her worst nightmare,
caught her as she fell into me.

There was no time to be
the mourning sister,
because if I had let her go,
she surely would have fallen apart,
cracked at the edges
and fallen to the floor
in a pile of sadness
and disbelief.

There were no words
of comfort I could speak,
no face I could paint onto myself
to make it easier.

Our mother sat,
willing everything inside of her
to pull you back here,
prayed to her god to let you go,
to return you.

When you didn't come,
she stopped praying
and didn't pray again
for a very long time.

1

You are gone now.
He delivered seventeen more blows
after the first one,
after the one that took you.

It's quiet now.
No more pain,
no more racing thoughts,
no more worry.

The rest were for us,
the left behind,
the still living
who mourn you
and miss you
and wish for you.

You are gone now
and the other seventeen
are the ghosts
we cannot escape,
the torture we relive.

Let me count it back for you.

About Kat Savage

Kat Savage resides in Louisville, Kentucky with her family of heathens. She's Slytherin, House Stark, and 99% sure her ancestors were pagan Viking Danes.

Kat Savage is a survivor of many ugly things and writes about them shamelessly in both poetry and novels.

Find more about Kat Savage on www.thekatsavage.com or stalk her on social media:

Facebook - /katsavagepoetry
Instagram - @katsavage

Join her reader group on Facebook – Kat's MF Savages – and be the first to know all her secrets.

Kat Savage would love it if you followed her Amazon author page and reviewed her work on Goodreads because it's very helpful to her as an indie author.

Kat Savages loves and adores you. You are important to her. Always.

Made in the USA
Middletown, DE
21 April 2020